Contemporary Greek Women Poets

Contemporary Greek Women Poets

translated by

Eleni Fourtouni

THELPHINI PRESS

Some of these poems were first published in "Connections," "City Lights Anthology—a Poetry Review," and "The Noiseless Spider."

The translator wishes to thank Bert Mathieu, who helped and encouraged her when this translation was first conceived.

Designed by Marcia Biederman and Robert Livingston

Typeset in Garamond No. 3
Display type in Della Robbia

Copyright © 1978 by Thelphini Press

No portion of this book may be reproduced without the written permission of the publisher, except by reviewers writing for the public press. Address inquiries to Thelphini Press, 1218 Forest Road, New Haven, Connecticut.

To my mother, my grandmother, and all the Greek women whose voices are unheard.

Contents

Translator's Introduction	ix
VICTORIA THEODOROU	1
RITA BOUMI-PAPPAS	15
MELPO AXIOTE	21
LILI BITA	29
KATERINA ANGHELAKI-ROOKE	35
KIKI DIMOULA	47
JENNY MASTORAKI	53
ELENI FOURTOUNI	61

Translator's Introduction

In 1974 I spent several months in Greece, which was then still controlled by the colonels' dictatorship.

The oppression was palpable, felt especially among students and writers. Wishing to contribute in some way to their struggle, I decided to translate young Greek poets whose voices, because of political insubordination, had been silenced.

I had no difficulty in discovering many poets whose work moved me deeply. But soon I realized that something was missing. Where are the women poets?—I asked. —There are none—was the answer I received from the avant-garde publisher who had given me a treasure-trove of works by men poets.

I inquired further among students, friends, academicians. Always there was the same answer—there is no important woman poet writing the kind of poetry you are looking for.

At last I found Nana, a woman in her mid 50's who had been involved in the resistance during the second world war, and who had paid the price for her struggle by her victimization during political witch-hunts. She owns the Kedros publishing house and a bookstore by the same name in Athens. She smiled when I told her of my problem, and showed me rows of shelves filled with slim volumes of poetry written by women.

The women whose work is included in this anthology, are not necessarily better poets than the many others I read. The choice was difficult, and I chose, not as a critic, but as a woman, protesting, searching, attempting to create. Their combined voices are a chorus, singing of our despair, our anger, our joy.

ELENI FOURTOUNI

Victoria Theodorou

Victoria Theodorou lives in Athens with her husband and two daughters. She was born in Greece of a Cretan mother and Yugoslavian father. She studied literature at the University of Athens. During World War II she participated in the resistance movement. For this she was shut in various island concentration camps for a period of five years by the rightist government which ruled Greece after the war.

The titled poems included in this anthology are selected from her book *Northern Suburb* published by Kedros in Athens. All other poems are taken from a book-length sequel, *Picnic*. This is an account of her return, twenty years later, to a place of exile, where she and hundreds of other women political prisoners lived under very harsh conditions for a number of years. These women, aged seventeen to seventy, some of whom had small children with them, chose exile rather than to sign a "declaration of repentance" repudiating their beliefs, struggles, and comrades, in order to be returned to their homes.

The names and situations cited in the poems are real.

PICNIC

1.

on these branches I left
my youth
at the crack of dawn I prowled
round these shrubs for mushrooms
four years I lived on
sea-watching
here I dug, over there I nailed
down poles for my tent
on bits of broken water-jugs
I wrote my verses
hiding them inside the hollow of trees

I've come back to look for them
twenty years later

2.

Against this wall
where they stood me up barefoot to take my measurements—
warm me now uplift me—
and here where I was pushed down—give me your hand
I'm light now and I wear a shirt as bright-red
as an aloe
come over here where they made me roll
the triple-thick barbed wire
wrap me in the velvet of your arms
and over here, where I lugged the cauldrons
and the ammunition cases

Here's the olive tree where I was getting the fifty grams
of bitter-tasting "dry nourishment," where I stood up
only to be shoved down
I placed on the linen cloth the bread
I made between two poems
here's roast meat, and nuts, and here's wine
Let's eat today, let's drink
for the hunger of those years.

3.

Here I lived with the other women prisoners
the canvas is rotten—and the ropes
not a trace left of the wall and the ditch
but the poles have sprouted. I know them
one of them's oak the other poplar
it's all written down on their leaves
and the leaves don't lie

Once again I see the snake near the wells
slithering from olive tree to olive tree
blocking the water
I see Saint George, monster killer, indifferent
inside this chapel, his spear made of paper
unmoved in his icon all those years
by the child's thirst
by the need of the bleeding mothers
Torrents have washed me, purified me
more merciful and consistent than health officers
deadly bacilli and dysentery germs have feared me
the earth innoculated me

Four winters
forbidden any fires for fear we'd flash signals
to the guerilla-filled mountains
How did we survive this?

4.

A fisherman's net forgotten in the sun—
a stretcher to carry uphill
a wounded woman
Aniouska are you still alive?
Vasso—with the fertile thighs
your children roam the streets
Rosa—with the fertile mind
Joy—you're forever mourning
Eleni—unadorned and unloved
Maria—the good word's late in coming
Dawn—dawn you're no longer
Aphrodite—the first star you left to us
Demeter from Thesaloniki
Elli of Kastro—come take your children
Grammatiki from Samos—with your books
you learned much, but
you were not content
Drosoula of Florida—here you saw
ships and harbors for the first time in your life
but I swear to you this isn't the way trips are taken
Thalia—weaver of seashells
save the poet with your dolphin
Froso—one-eyed from a bullet
on the left, Ephrosini with the clear gaze
on the right, a broken statue of a Kore
tightrope-walkers walking down the path

5.

When the whale spat me out on this beach
I was too dazed to understand their warning
carved on the cliffs. Too sick to be afraid.
"Hope for nothing" it read.
Later, when I took in its meaning
I scorned it
Hope! what use is it to me, I thought.
The sea will stand by me
and the olive tree
I am not the first to taste exile
But I will be the last.
I will abolish it with my life.
I swear.

6.

A yellow flag on the west peninsula
declaring typhus
come out of the wells
the indifferent flies buzz all over
on whose tent will he squat . . .

he's chosen Natalia's little girls
Olga and Thespina
stay away from Company A
call the doctor, go kowtowing to him
so he might have mercy on us
We've been, we've bowed and scraped and cried
He called us hysterical, out of our minds
he slammed the door in our faces

The yellow flag's flapping and threatening
the caique's tied down fast to the breakwater
the captain drinks with the policemen
the gramophone's roaring
the women are pleading . . .
—There'll be no more trips today, ladies. Tomorrow
the health officer will be here—
Tomorrow . . .

7.

Women, disdainful, uncaring
bridegrooms waiting
urging and threatening
biting on the ring of their fate
the winds scatter their desire
the women are drunk on the wild honey of solitude

The sound of the bugle scatters the larks
it stabs and terrorizes the peaceful Centaurs
it snuffs out the dreams of dawn, burns
the bridges
Leaden legs hold up the body
—beaten and humiliated—
heavy boots hold up the spirit
    on these collapsing cliffs
and this gravel

8.

Slender, unrepenting women
harvesting shells by the sea
Irma, Aliki, Athena, Louisa
the unsubdued, the dreamers
Gods, they disdained you—
don't get even with them

Strength spent on the ax
splitting wood in the kitchens
hair washed for Holy Thursday
dried by the harsh wind, unperfumed
tied down
in cheap cheesecloth
ardor humiliated by hunger
will throttled by wrangling
ideals diseased by discord
hard night
dawn will make no difference.

Victoria Theodorou

9.

Women by the thousands were walled-in
in this empty, nameless island
—officially declared unfit for human habitation
infested with yellow fever and typhus—
We were the first to camp here
on this meager soil we worked, we gave birth
we buried, we sang
we abolished emptiness
we built kilns and workshops
wells and windmills
here we lived out the clay age
we dug for roots
we coaxed the music from the reed
we made a lyre from the turtle shell

10.

Renoula, Popi, Titika, Melpo
their names—singing birds
morning-glories and evening flowers—
a cruel god turned them into dark, grim masks
dressed them in coarse cloth
tents of khaki, olive trees of khaki
    sea of khaki and sky of khaki
not a single flower left
a blood-red ribbon for their wild hair

". . . send me colored silks and linen
and Itzedin's guitar—
hide a knife inside the case—
leather, candles, good twine
and all the paper you can . . ."

GALATIA KAZANZAKI

Freed from the island-camp
I walked the city streets—lost
she took me in
she gave me bread and wine
she made my bed with her precious rugs
embroidered with deer and falcons
out of her gloom she gave me light
determination to write my verse
on the ring she put on my finger she etched
her message
—Make a song out of life's pain—

OLD SONG

They threw her body on a stretcher
arms dragging on the gravel
the tassle of her braid—a golden broom
sweeping the road to the river
around her the mocking mob
pokes at her belly.
They made our mothers come out
to see her shame
to see what's in store for us—
their rebel daughters—
celebrating her death in our mountains. But
the women cried and sang for her
they washed the slime from her face
tenderly they closed her visionary's eyes
they told her story to the reeds.

A passing poet will sing her song
I am only a sparrow inside the river reeds
I don't sing, I don't cry
I don't forget
I have marked the site with my nest
I don't leave for the winter.

NUYEN TI SOY

She's walking all alone in the jungle
a machete in one hand
to cut down branches
and startle away poisonous snakes—
in the other, her gun. Between her breasts
grenades.
She's come to set traps far away from her comrades.
She's become a beast in the jungle
She's weaving traps with slender fingers
that also know how to embroider lotus flowers
and birds-of-paradise.
Her slenderness, her frail strength, know the fear
of formidable men armed to the teeth with the arts of war
She knows the whole jungle, step-by-step—
her brothers had planned to make a farm there
She's stepping along the rice paddies, she's hiding
she's stalking, she's crawling in the mud of the rice paddies—
her hands hold her gun up, dry
her white teeth hold her braid, clean
and deep in her heart
she holds her death

Rita Boumi-Pappas

Rita Boumi-Pappas is a poet of great renown and enormous productivity. Her first book of poems, published in 1930, was followed by sixteen other publications.

The four poems translated here are selected from her book *A Thousand Murdered Girls*. They are about young women in the Greek resistance during World War II, who were summarily courtmartialed and executed when they refused to sign "declarations of repentance and good behavior."

The poems consist, in essence, of what the young women wrote and said before they died, as transmitted to the poet by her husband, Nikos Pappas, who acted as attorney for the defense.

In her introduction, Rita Boumi-Pappas writes—These executed girls are my daughters, your daughters, the daughters of all real people. They fell, not only for political freedom, but for personal freedom, for the right as individuals to choose. They did not die to be silent.

MARIA R.

Well then, it's all over. The case
my future prospects
the anxiety about the outcome of the trial

Yesterday they announced my sentence:
"Death!"

I don't have to bother about it anymore.
Now I can even say that I got through it
successfully.
I expected it to be drawn-out, exhausting,
and tragic.

Nothing like that.
The whole thing lasted five minutes.
Their docket is crowded with
the names of comrades
waiting to be convicted.

I'm suddenly filled with peace, my friends!
Even joy. It looks like some of the men
will get out—you know I've a weakness for them
I'm glad I stuck to my guns. I feel it's right
for our struggle.

So, I'm on "death row!"
It seems like a funny thing—even if it is
dead serious—I'm not big enough for it.
Even so, it makes me proud, stubborn.
It makes me a rock.

And I'll spit on their decision—
this scrap of paper that kicks me
out of life at 19—I'll step on it like
the stub of their cigar
before I go.

KRINIO

Aim straight at my heart
it has served me well up to now.
to make it easy for you
I've sewn this black piece of cloth
right in the middle of my breasts.

I don't know what your fire will be like
—poor beardless soldiers—they've got you up
at dawn on my account
I've never held a gun—I don't know

I see your eyes wide open
—you can't help all this—
your hands want to touch me
before they pull the trigger—I understand

You probably still have the nicknames
of your boyhood
and who knows, we might've played together in the streets

Go on, spare me the morning frost
I'm almost naked
dress me in your fire
smile at me boys
cover my body with your gaze

I've never been covered by a lover
not even in dream . . .

ARTEMIS

This road I'm taking is long and bright
and cold
walking it at dawn, barefoot . . .

In prison I prepared for this trip
Women on death row stayed up all night with me
they gave me a change of clean clothes
and perfumed soap
they sprinkled rose water on my hair
and when they waved goodbye
they promised that it wouldn't be long
before we met again
from the iron-barred windows
they shouted—wait for us

Where am I?
which way is Kilkis and our house?
which way is the blue lake of Thoirani
I saw for the first time on a school outing?
I don't know this place
but my blood will be spilled here—
like wine in a wedding—
You get your guns ready—yawning
(don't hold it against me for waking you so early)
I comb my hair for the last time

Go on! hurry, what are you waiting for?
you want to know my last wish?

I'm 19. I don't want to die.

ERASMINA

I wasn't afraid of death
I walked tall with him
between two rows of guns
and silent, bent soldiers.
My head was pounding
when I howled over the open ditch—
loud enough for even the deaf to hear
"I'm innocent"
nobody believed me. My scream
didn't break the wall
the wind kept blowing
and the city was unmoved.

Perea, workers of 5 A.M.
factory—where I was locked for twelve hours every day
mother, house, winter cold
small mirror, shining like noon
when I'd look in you
my 20 year old hope, standing against this wall
—at 5 A.M.—that same hour—
and with the same work dress!

Who will sing?
who will collect
what is coming to me
what I've lost
and for which they shoot me down?

Melpo Axiote

Melpo Axiote published her first novel in 1938. Other novels, books of poetry, critical studies, and translations followed.

Melpo, who was a firm believer in human freedom, made her life and work an example of resistance against tyranny. Her funeral in the summer of 1974 sparked a demonstration for life and freedom in the streets of junta-controlled Athens.

The Homestead is taken from a collection of her poems, published by Kedros in Athens. It is a nightmarish, surrealistic poem describing women trying to live in a man-made world.

THE HOMESTEAD

Katerina, Rotho, and Theano wear their heavy dresses.
It's raining cats and dogs.
Mountains and trees are shrinking, the rooster returns
on the rooftop, things are turning hard, and the light around
        people is dimming.
Even the house is shivering.
Katerina, Rotho, and Theano shut the north windows tight.
The waves are trying to beat down the gate, the fire shrivels
in terror deep into the ashes.
Nearby an old cat is dreaming strange stories.
Katerina, Rotho, and Theano wait calmly for Spring.

They know
the house is an old-timer, and this storm will pass
if they're meant to go on here.

On a sunny morning when everything was open and clear
the sea caught sight of a strange pair of eyes.
—Oh, that's the last bridegroom—the sea said
—you see, he's quite intact, he's new here—
The bridegroom went on down, unaware, like a diver. A lovely
gold chain dangling from his vest pocket,
shining under water, and a school of fish followed
after it,
eagerly trying to nibble on it—but the bridegroom was quite
        unconcerned.
He went unaware, down the path
traced out by the sea currents, he went on
apparently traveling on his own momentum, down that silent
        road to America.

It was almost noon, and time was dragging on,
when they received Philip for the first time in the parlor.

—Did you have a nice trip?—the first sister asked.
—Yes did you—asked the second.
—Did you have a nice trip?—the third asked quickly.
Philip had brought a letter from their brother, Manoli, in
    California.
—Was it far, the place where you met him?—
—Yes was the place far?—
—Was it far?—
The sun, swinging round the house, settled on a single spot;
everything else was in half darkness
and nothing in the world mattered. Only those three women
dressed in brown, holding, one after another, the brother's letter
at the point where it said
        —and Philip will marry
Katerina in mid-December—
The sisters fell to thinking.
Looking out through the north window,
one after the other whispering
        —What secret
does the sea hold? What answer?
We know nothing, we're three
women. We don't know—
And they laughed, like masks
made of cheap village cloth
        —even the house agreed.

Tonight a window shines in the dark sky—a bad omen
to birds
who fly to hiding places.
—Dearest, what's wrong with your hands? What's happened to
    them?
They've grown so
old! Oh your poor hands, they've grown so old . . . says the first
    voice.
—Well . . . my hands have grown old . . . ? I haven't
    noticed—says the second voice.
—Come, dearest, I'll take you to bed. You've been standing
for so long. You'll be tired—

Rotho knits nearby.
The spool drags on the floor.
The yarn is tangled around the leg of her chair.
The cat takes hold of it and drags it round even more—
this undercurrent of sound makes the heavy silence
even louder in the house.
—Ach!—Katerina says suddenly
—there's a smell of warmed-over lunch in the air.
    Just think. When we were still human
we used to enjoy the world's stench. But now
—Katerina laughed—now everything's too much—
years have passed since then . . . I wonder if anyone has counted
    them—
—No—replies Theano
    —we can't know that
Everything moves so softly around us it's not
easy to calculate. But
that night, without a doubt,
all three of us were wearing our brown dresses—
—Yes yes, that's right—says Katerina—our brown
dresses. Tonight
I think I can see a thin sliver of the world—
Katerina feels the walls with her fingernails and listens.
Behind her blind eyes, her mind tricks her into seeing
all those confusing events of her past life, quite clearly.
—Yes yes—she says
—I see well tonight.
We had a hard time. We always wanted to do
what other people around us did.
But you see—Katerina laughs—we weren't really
people then. and of course we didn't realize it right away.
But it seems now
as if we've always been dolls . . .
—Bring the teacup—says Theano.
—Don't mess up the floor with your tears—
Rotho brings over the copper cup with the sleek bird in the
    middle and sits down again.

[24]

—To tell the truth, I'm glad—Katerina goes on—I'm not sorry I
   lived.
      Except that
the Venetian mirror broke in all the confusion.
—What . . . ! says Theano.
—Oh yes, that large carved mirror of ours.
I remember. Maybe
that's why we've lost track of the years since then.
None of us has gone back in the parlor to see herself in the mirror
   since that night—
—No—screams Katerina—I don't need that. I had seen the
   world too well
then. I know everything by heart.
I don't want to see anymore.
Give me your hand
I want to walk—

Katerina gropes to the other side, and she ends up near the left
corner, next to the wall
      next to the darkness.
—Tonight we must talk—she says—
—we must say something about that wasted life of ours tonight,
while we can still see.
It will be over by morning
She bows slightly and keeps on talking
—Please come right in—don't be afraid.
You must have come a long way. How was your trip, are you
   tired?
She moves a little to the side, as if to let someone pass by.
—Well of course I know you. You really think
I don't remember that your name is
Philip and that I was married to you once?
And now
I suppose you've come to see your child.
But you won't see it.
Because I never had a child.
Are you upset now?

Since the child was in my own womb I had the right to do with it
 as I pleased. Don't you agree?
Oh come now, don't be angry
Your hair will fall off . . .
Interrupting her, a voice nearby says
—Katerina, dearest
sit down for a while. You'll be too tired—
—Please be quiet—says Katerina tensely—I've got to welcome
 Philip, don't you see?
You'll get me all confused
and I won't have time to finish—and she goes on
—yes, we're all dolled up—as you can see.
Our brown dresses.
They're our best, and we kept
waiting—thinking you might come back.
Would you like me to show you his little things now? Look—
and Katerina goes through the motions of opening up her apron
and taking out the child's clothes, piece by piece.
—They're lovely, aren't they? We were sewing for one hundred
 and one days and nights.
I was pregnant for many, many months . . . The people who
 came
said it would be a boy for certain.
But I gave birth to no child—
Once again the voice nearby says—Katerina,
dearest, sit down for a while. You'll get too tired.

The lamp with its broad wick keeps smoking. He comes in
at the low side-door, facing west.
Katerina, Rotho, and Theano
step forward to see.
They raise the lamp up high to see the man better.
—What do you want—they ask the man.
—Who killed him—he asks.
—I killed him—said Katerina. And the three
can see they are speaking into the dead silence
with their blind-all-seeing eyes.
 —Still, that

time long ago when we too were people, I think
we had a brother. And he might be this one. The sea
was always taking and sending them back . . . It's better,
sisters, not to care for anything—
        —Why should we care now?
Let him suffer. He's the one who lost us.
He could have had us.
Now we're only three quite harmless
        mechanical dolls—
Then it was time for the rats to come out for their nightly prowl
        in the house.
—Bring bread—ordered Katerina—there's no reason
to forget them just because we have a guest—
—What have you done with him—he shouted.
And the rats came scuttling out of their holes in droves,
at regular intervals, filling the room. Some swung from the
        curtains
some gathered round the lamp. Some circled round Katerina's
        hand
some darted over to the corner towards three pairs of gray,
        worn-out slippers.
They gnawed on things unconcerned
        like some old habit
come out for a stroll.
—The sea took him—said Katerina.
        —He came the night
we were wearing our brown dresses. We
knew him at once. We marked him out
the time he came to marry me.
And our Venetian carved mirror broke in the confusion, just
        before the sea
took him.
We haven't seen him since—

Gradually as Katerina talked on, she hunched over, little
by little, and fell
asleep.

Melpo Axiote

He took off his black
shoes. Holding them
in his hands, he
turned down the lamp,
and stepping quietly he backed out.

Lili Bita

Lili Bita transcends the individual woman—wrote Anaïs Nin of her and her work.

Lili's life, a constant struggle to transcend the limitations of being merely human, is filled with her passion for people and poetry.

Born on the island of Zante, she studied music and drama in Athens. She emigrated to the United States, where she thrives as a poet, playwright, and actress.

She has published five books of poetry, one novel, a translation of Anaïs Nin's *A Spy in the House of Love*, and numerous plays.

She lives in Miami with her husband, poet Robert Zeller, and one of her two sons.

PORTRAIT
For Eleni

Woman with the body of a lesbian
or of a satyr
I watch you suffer in your attempt
to become the arrow that will
match your spirit
in your endless highs
Now is Greece. Light.
That yellow blaze entering
the arteries of things
to make them immortal.
Now there're sandy beaches
and salt-eaten rocks.
Now there's the taste of your own sex
in your mouth.
Now you sink
deeper than memory
now you're the image
of sick rooms
of oxygen tents
of bedpans in terminal wards
now you're the echo of your own
death rattle.
But the helter-skelter chorus at the
crossroads has judged you
faithless, insatiable, barren.
As you sink in the blazing
skull of silence
the helter-skelter lovers
trap you in their blind fingers.

We live in their prisons, Woman.

THE BARBARIAN

Tonight I regret
the peace
the tender looks and the soft caresses
the balm of pity, the sigh of compromise
small talk, lukewarm sex
the stubborn chastity
of our mingling flesh
tonight I want you
barbarian in my bed
with no conscience and no hope
with no limits and no regrets
with the torch of the phallus
in your eyes
with the world's sour sweat on your body
with the wombs of all women
in your hands
with the sword of the conqueror
between your thighs
fire for fire, lust for lust
tonight I want you—Demon
and no man inside me.

WOMB

A marvel of design
woven with precious
intricate membranes
the prize and the riddle
of the body
every month blood slips
weblike
from its depths on sterilized
white cotton pads
every night
in dream or fact
it throbs with
pleasure
like the dial
of the cardiogram
convulsively.

THE BLOOD CRIMINAL

I am a blood-priestess
a criminal exalted in her crimes
I free the outlaw riders of my spirit
women, sisters
press your hands on the life-giving spring
smear the white-washed kitchens
the vapid faces of your lovers
everything that denies the dark sign of
its birth
when you lay naked under the male lust
open wide the bleeding cunt
the powerful hot smell
the rich thick flow, the lumpy pulp

my legions, my stallions, my lovers!
all loving is good
fear is the only perversion

Katerina Anghelaki-Rooke

Katerina Anghelaki-Rooke was born in Athens where she still lives with her husband, half of the time. The other half she spends in her house at Aegina, writing poetry, cultivating her pistachio orchard, and healing her friends' wounds with her laughter and love.

Seferis said—the one basic subject of poets is their own living body. Katerina's poetry is a celebration of her body's joy and anguish. Life, love, pain are for her a gift. She lives with it and makes poetry out of it.

KATERINA ANGHELAKI-ROOKE

MY MAMA AND SATAN

On Good Friday
Virgin Mary becomes again the belle of the ball
and my mamma's no longer made of marble.
She no longer wears that pink
they buried her in
and she doesn't necessarily go down
with her box.
On Good Friday
my mamma alive, warm as candle
wears some old thing or other.
Her fingernail fatty at the edges, like mine
—the next-to-the-last-one—
A stranger
thinking in secret
sinning in secret
far from me
plotting her endless death
SHE TORTURES ME.
What have I done wrong
what mistake did I make
what ritual did I neglect?
Grim the Easter of memory
life is again nailed
on the cross
the lilac cuts through me
stretched out on the black and white tiles
I lament
in the sacrament of time
I've had no time
I will have no time
to find the mistake
before Resurrection.

City by the sea
mamma can't stand the damp
it's raining raining raining

the jetty's a grain of lentil in the drizzle
restricted lives
fully planned
two streets of passion
three neighborhoods of dreams
and summer
sticks to you
like the spit of always the same
five people.
Clumsy age
miserable days
seasonal sicknesses
they walk around
with their tics, with their faces
everything familiar
as their name.
Mamma—
well-attended funeral
hats and parties
stories just don't reveal you
they only label you
they place you, mention you
but I want the inner, inner, inner
the insideness of the skin
the little gadget of your breath
and that other thing
the obsessive dread
in your thinking.
How much goodness in you
how much rust
how much natural peace.

Male crane
you turn me on
under your forehead
is the devil's blue
the blue of alcohol
the puritan blue.

KATERINA ANGHELAKI-ROOKE

Blood and calves
purified by dust
going down with the setting sun
the cannibalistic sunset
of the docksides
center of slaughter
sulphurous.

You caress me
with your awe
a knife swaddled in rags
a knight who lost his horse in the battle
of the backyard.
The dream is
like an upside-down coffee cup
we touch it
it sweats inside
it drips roads
pine-planted destinies
I tell fortunes
you tell fortunes
together we invent my mamma
this one, right here
sweeter
more enticing
she feeds me on guilt
my whole life.
Enslaved
I touch you
I cover with my palm
your whole face
I want.
My mamma did she ever want
or did she always sigh
in silence
with all the—I wants—piled deep
at the back of her throat?

The sun falls
in a blood-soaked ditch

and the moon with bright porcupine spikes
still resists.
The sky's a dried-up pit
like a hungry bitch's tits.
If only I had some small passion
like the old woman with the paper bag
who slips in the park
in rain or snow
to feed the cats.

But love is a large bag
shut tight
and in it animals kicking
nightmares.
Like something out of place
you're hard to believe
weak, shriveled flesh
I need you
the struggle must be revived
mother-desire
mother-passion.
You wear the mask
that says—I'll always be gone
the flour-mask of death
a red thread for mouth
but I made you up, you can't affect me
that's how it's got to be
to be guilty again
to get the taste of it again
Eleni, Eleni,
The lovely chant is forgotten
and the secret seasons of the house
When the house, cut off from the future
breathes in unison
with the things
with the comings and goings of the faithful.
These detailed memories are awful
they're carapaces

with the sea monster gone
I'm giving up childhood
I'm daring destruction
I don't consider the body
a precious entity.
And that's when she appears
from inside the landscape I've deformed
she appears
spreading her evening Nivea on her face
shocked
she watches me as I slip into
sinful regions.
It's raining
I've come out
maledictions are pouring down on me
I've come out
I take the risk.

Restless
restless with the rolling rocks
restless with the hallucinatory colors
restless with the radiant morning animals
when they sing out
—again, always, the end—
restless with the poem
I dig up childhood
I dig up adolescence
I dig up my mother's belly
with Caesar's sword.
But I'm encircled
with Nature's beauty
the way every plant fills
with its own death
the space between brown and blue.
Archangelic endings
painful highs
I marvel at the only immortal I know—
the day—

I marvel
but I fall in love
with what's behind Karaghiozis' screen
the immense longing
when what I've lost
and what I'll never know
are lost in the same shadow.

Mamma's heirs are
the things
I rub my nose
on them
like the cat that pees in the **parlor**—
repentent
I swallow my spittle
and run up to hide
inside the staircase
inside the immense feline
I climb up
it kicks me off
I hang on
it spits me out
the landing's on fire
the ropes are burning
around the rim of the dark hole
scarabs are crowding.
 Mother I'm in danger
  —your memory is everlasting
 Mother I'm in danger
  —your memory is everlasting.

MAGDALEN THE GREAT MAMMAL

I pass my life
through the eye of the same rusty
old needle
and I sew, I sew my passion.
The wrinkles on my belly
like city streets
the square with its obelisk
everything familiar
and myself familiar but ignorant.
I only know myself in sex
and what defeats me in sex—
a cliché that sings.
Tricked out with the seasons
I switch dresses
and the body
changes shapes
with the weather
I blow it up each morning
and the balloon-vendor takes off
with the pump.

I begin with an itching in the middle
of the palm
a nail or a brutal fly
whose triangular snout rubs against
the dark counterpart
the fear—like the root's fear—
that the air will rot
that the earth will harden
that the end will take root.
And look, I'm playing jump-rope in the sky
I'm eating with the fiends
masqueraded as cows with
grassy dreams
I plan to prove nothing with my life
that's why I fell in love with you

I, a mammal of a future
prehistory
poisoned from so much sperm
I ruminate on the futile words
of my act
—always play-acting as if I were to
die soon—
that's why I fell in love with you.
Our time is short
we'll both survive
the unailing
I, dragging
my time-wrecked body
and you, always beaming
steeped in
childlike songs
—Christ,
you're beautiful
and your name is hard
like resin
but everything else about you
is soft.
Your heart roves
like the sea
around all the islands.

The cranes in the harbor
are lugging up the night
little feathered clouds
of the holy hen
open up the day to the waters.
On the deserted pier
I wait—a hunk of darkness
cut out of dark rock
I wait to be taken in a dark carriage
or else break with light.
There's always some soft spot
on this earth

for us homeless
in the final moment.
There was no resurrection for us
no resistance
there was no act
we just roosted
hopelessly bundled up in cloths
too cumbersome for lovemaking
moaning faintly through damp noses
frozen in the chill.
You'll head for the skies
as if you had no body
you'll go up in light
in spite of dreaming the photographer's darkroom.
You're going off to the nightingale's winters
and I spread you out with my fingers
a shadow on the eucalyptus-lined street.
I press my whole body
on your whole body
and I try to believe in your death
—As for my own . . . it is difficult—
the way the yellow darkens
in the dusk
when the hidden smell hits you
and the flower is only a stigma.
The green almond will ripen
passion will turn into belief
in time . . .
Belief nests inside me
with minute movements I love
what is
and what can never be.
What a marvelous affair
the burning bush!
It's forever burning
in a landscape just like my skin
something between desolate yellow
and the mute green of fertility.
I suffer. I suffer with

the whole world
suddenly the truth is clear
in the words of the dead.
I press your navel
and I expand emptiness.
Through sex I learn
what a burden you'll always be carrying
—god or stranger—
And I take your body
I take your watered-down blood
I'm ravaged by so many contradictions
I worship the enchantment
the traces of your teeth
on our old apple.
I am a hollow
fragrant with incense
what you are is forever
what I am ends here
here I stay
a matchless footprint
in the divine endlessness.

Kiki Dimoula

Kiki Dimoula lives and works in Athens. She is a bank employee, a wife, and of course a poet. Her first book of poetry, published in 1952, has been followed by four others.

The poems in this anthology were selected from her book *The Smallness of the World*, published by the author in Athens.

Her theme is usually of people condemned to remain outside the stream of life. But Kiki is, as an artist and as a woman, a vital element in that stream.

Kiki Dimoula

MARK OF RECOGNITION
Statue of a woman with hands tied

Right away they call you a statue.
I see you right away as a woman.

You decorate some park.
From a distance, you're misleading.
You seem to be slowly sitting up to remember
a lovely dream
gathering all your strength to live it out.
From close up, the dream clears away.
Your hands are tied behind you
with a rope of marble
and your whole bearing's taut with the will
to break out.
But that's the way their commission to the sculptor read
—captive—
You can't even
weigh a few raindrops in your hands,
or pick a daisy.
And the marble isn't your only Argus.
If changes were to take place
in the malleability of marble, if statues
were to start struggling
for freedom and equality—
like wage-slaves,
like the dead,
like our inner feelings—
you would still exist
inside this cosmogony of marble
with your hands still tied—captive—

They all call you a statue right away.
Right away I call you a woman
Not because the sculptor
surrendered you to the marble
as a woman
and your thighs promise generations

of beautiful statues
—a clean harvest of immobility—
But because your hands are tied.
Everywhere I turn
I see your hands are always
tied.
That's why I call you a woman.

I call you a woman
because you always end up
        a captive

TIED DOWN

The sea of Scaramaga—tied down
thick—black smoke from the oil tankers
hangs over it
A dirty cloud smudging the road up ahead
Down here, good intentions are again put off—
The horse will stay tied down
My mind—full of ties, full of knots
—let's say you exist—
In the car mirror
I see a dried-up well
In the fields, signs of fresh
digging—the same care
for corpses as for seeds.
At Mycenae—tombs and exclamations
Rocks tormented by renown
The passions of the mighty—memorable
No tourist will notice our passions
Oblivion waits around—ravenous
—let's say you exist—
At Nauplion—another white ship
Not really a ship and not really white
We leave the ambiguities behind
We walk among the bamboos
the lemon-trees, the cypresses
Fecund images—I water you
Far up the hill
a coal-train is chugging along
like a deliverance falling apart
—let's say you exist—
like limitless supplies of water
in uninhabited places
Like good omens inside
Stuffed birds
      —superfluous

Kiki Dimoula

TALKING TO MYSELF

It's all over—I told you
and you said
—don't worry about it
let go quietly
learn how to look at the stopped clock
       with self-composure
be sensible
realize it's not winding it needs
admit it—it's your life
       moving that way—
and don't you be fooled by occasional movements of the hands
it's got nothing to do
       with you
come on down
dethrone yourself soberly
you were only taking a chance
       at it
forget about it—smile

you had your say

STANDSTILL
A painting of a young woman in a coffee-shop

It's been years since she arrived
from the USA
inside some sailor's sack
and offered to the walls of the coffee-shop
winter and summer
        —framed—
Winters
    the land-locked lusts
        of sailors
bending over card games
manage to stir something inside her

but by summer
    it's all over
the coffee-shop is empty
with only an occasional swimmer
coming for a lemonade
or an ageing lady
    looking for shelter
        away from so much light.

In the thick silence
the framed woman demands
    her old age
—behind her a huge moon
    is wasted—

Jenny Mastoraki

Jenny Mastoraki is in her late twenties and the mother of a two-year-old daughter. She is determined to integrate her family and artistic life and not to allow her identity as an individual and as a poet to be diminished, nor to take the traditional second place in her life as a married woman.

In the midst of much family opposition, she finished the University of Athens with honors in philosophy and became committed to being a poet.

The following poems are selected from her first book, *Right of Passage*, published by Kedros in Athens. It was written as a protest against the oppressive seven years of military dictatorship in Greece.

Jenny, an active participant in the resistance against the junta, was among the students who fought during the uprising at the Polytechnic Institute in 1973. She was brutally beaten by the police, and she almost died as a result of internal hemorrhaging caused by that beating.

JENNY MASTORAKI

This silence I've nurtured
inside four walls
was meant to become a
song—
song deep and dark
like speechless water,
like the pocket in my mother's apron—
to give each her own
to spread like the message of the cranes
in the streets, in the squares
in the public urinals
in waiting-rooms
song like the mass on Palm Sunday
song of bread and water
song of the people
my song

HOW DID IT HAPPEN?

How did we get to this place, anyway?
What did we put into it and what are we getting out of it?
We're lugging on our backs
a name that doesn't belong to us—
endless roads
that were never our own.
They examine us like a new shoe
that someone else is wearing
while we were dreaming
of huge leaps over the seas—
in drought, you drink—as if to say
look, but don't you touch!
How did they come to squander us this way?
we paid out every last dime to them
in withholdings!
we who never owned much in the first place
gave up all our rights in advance . . .

Jenny Mastoraki

HOW I MANAGED TO SQUARE THE CIRCLE OF DREAMS IN THE SHAPE OF A WINDOW AT THE TOP OF THE STAIRS IN A TENEMENT HOUSE

a. The Poet

The poet's work
has simply got to be difficult.
Personally, I know nothing about it.
My whole life long's been spent
writing long, desperate letters
about drought-stricken neighborhoods
which I've sealed
inside bottles
and chucked down the sewers.

b. Birth

I sprouted in a hothouse
made of concrete.
The voice of a cow feeds around
inside my intestines.
I've limited myself in such a
vegetable state.
I haven't spoken.
I haven't provoked anyone.
I've always simply thrived
in places
where dictionaries consistently
denied my existence.

c. Marble Busts

I don't know what I would've done
if things hadn't turned out
this way.
I might've written
history books
for the third grade.
And then again I might've supervised pebbles in public parks.
In either case
the hands are useless.
I'm always bumping
against marble busts.

JENNY MASTORAKI

d. Theorem

Now then, I've shown you
how I managed to square
the circles of dreams
in the shape of a window
at the top of the stairs
in a tenement house.
This modest ceremony's over.
      You're asked
      to disperse
      quietly.

Jenny Mastoraki

The day's gone
and you're left with a telephone coin,
not knowing who to call
to say
that outdoors the sunset's scattering
proclamations
to the weathervanes.
You're left with a scrap of paper
clutched in the hand
on it a mangled message.
So you stand there with the coin in your palm
You stare at it: on one side
a profile of Justice
on the other, the herald's wand of Hermes—
symbols whose meanings
you can't even begin to see.

Eleni Fourtouni

Eleni Fourtouni was born in Sparta, Greece. In 1953 she came to the United States as an exchange student. She studied social studies at Nasson College in Springvale, Maine. Soon after graduation she married and devoted the next fifteen years of her life to raising her son and daughter. Eventually she became interested in other things, especially women and their place in the world.

She plans a study on women and crime in Greece, and is presently translating nine journals kept by Greek women political prisoners during the war in Greece. The journals have been compiled and published by the poet Victoria Theodorou, an inmate of the camp and a writer of one of the journals.

ELENI FOURTOUNI

CHILD'S MEMORY

Every time I think of it
there's a peculiar tickle
on my throat
especially when I clean fish—
the fish my blond son brings me
proud of his catch—
and I must cut off the heads

my hand
holding the blade
hesitates
that peculiar tickle again
I set aside the knife
fleetingly I scratch my throat
I bring the knife
down
on the thick scaly neck—
not much of a neck really
just below the gills—
I hack at the slippery hulk of bass
my throat itches
my hands stink fish
they drip blood
my knife cuts through

the great head is off
I breathe

once again the old image comes
into focus
the proud, blond soldier
his shining black boots
his spotless green uniform

smiling
he lugs a sack
into the schoolyard

the children, curious, gather
he dips his ruddy hand inside the sack
the children hold their breath

what is it, what?
he must have been in our gardens again
looting the cabbage
the children think
their brown hands
fly to their eyes
No
we mustn't look
at it
it's too horrible

but we're full of curiosity
between our spread fingers
we see . . .

the soldier's laughter is gleefully loud
as he pulls out
the heads of two Greek partisans

quickly I rinse the blood off my knife

EURYNOME

I feared your wrath Eurynome
my grandmother
when your ancient gnarled fingers
would reach to my child's
thighs, pinching obedience into
my flesh—my flesh
spawned from your
rebellious flesh

the hearth's too narrow
for the likes of you
from first light to last light
you roam your valleys
and scale your mountains
commanding fields to yield good harvest
      vineyards to grow sweet fruit
          saplings to turn into olive trees
the ravines resounding with
your song, your anger
with the first cry of your babes
born next to your
plow

you take death as you take life
with huge leaps and bounds
grieving
over the graves of your
children
eating from the fiery fruit
of the dead
to burn away your pain

leading the dance-circle again
with the black banner
of your mourning
you feed the beggars at your door
the guests at your table
you oversee
your storerooms with rows of
clay jars filled with olive oil
goat skins packed with cheese
wine caskets fermenting new wine
your power
spilling over, into
the dark dough of our
daily bread

you fed me
the black broth you brewed
from your
blood
briney olives and thyme honey
grandmother
and when you sat by the
west window, taking in
the Last Light
you gave me your last command

"Give to no man
your Time of Life."

PAPPOULI

You no longer cared to know us
but you knew Taygetos
to the end

for thirty-four thousand days
the mountain filled your eyes
with shimmering blue—
etched inside your now closed eyelids—
always blending in perfect chaos
and harmony—the two of you
told each other stories
and the mountain taught you how to be
wise and patient

you knew the change in the weather
by the way the light
reflected on the cliffs
you knew how long it was before daybreak
by the distance between
the morning star and
the snow-covered peaks
you knew the sun well
as it paused on the mountain-rim
for a friendly farewell

you wanted to know
what was even beyond your line of vision
over the rim
you waited
you knew the sun would pull you
behind Taygetos
you knew you'd see
the light-filled crags

today the sun decided you have waited enough

IN A DREAM

You were standing in the garden
your garden
no, you were not putting seeds in the soft earth
no, you were not pruning the vines
no, you were not taking in the smells and the visions
wearing black, you stood against the gray wall
the monstrous bird beside you
man-sized
shrouding you in his wings
a bridegroom

LAMENT

when you were dying
I turned my eyes away
your last breath was too horrible
your body
deformed in death
repugnant

(your other daughter closed your eyes)

when did I stop touching you?
how long before you died
did your hands, swollen and unbending
lay lonely at your side?

my warm, supple fingers
could make the frown of pain disappear

why did I stop touching you

that morning
when I came early
a nurse stopped me at the door
don't be frightened dear—the eyes, the bleeding
it's only a punctured blood vessel

two red tears
like the rubies on your ring
(the one Maria kept)

the mountains that stand around Vassara
still stand. Green

you are dead

and yet their existence
had always guaranteed that you could not die
I thought the mountains needed you
but they are getting along fine
without you

I am not a mountain

HOMECOMING

I walk in your house and see your loneliness
the sun-filled rooms echo your gaze
searching for traces of your life
watching me
endlessly hesitating
endlessly
squandering my longings

you never sent me that message
you never warned me that our time
was running out

your garden
the orange trees are shading it
their roots reach deep
they keep me near you
breathing your love and plenty

I smell your spices simmering
I see your blue skirt
I see your face
etched on the Olive Trees

I HAVE NO POEM FOR YOU FATHER

In life, you came
now and then
your valise full of
city-smells. The smell
of wine
in your hair
Your visits, landmarks
marked
by her welcome

I loved to see you
come
to see our house hung in
flowers
I loved the honey-cakes she made
the washed floorboards, rinsed
with yellow stain

And I loved to see you
go, father

In death
I saw you, not at all

You spared me all that
with the ocean you put
between your cancer-bed
and me, six months away
from your grave
when you smiled and gave me
to the sea

I gave no tears
no thoughts

no poems to you
father

I scarcely heard
the voice untangling
bringing me your message:

to keep myself, to scale
Taygetos
to fathom the deep
    to grow wings
        to grow fins, to sing my song

I walk the earth
still, and I have no song
for you father

PARTING

I wrapped my eyeballs
in soft cloth and tucked them away
they will not look at
you again

my two lips
I buried in the dust
now they thirst only for water

my swift feet
rest among the cobwebs
your door is thousands of miles
from here

my arms
are hidden in the snow
they can never hold you
back

I should have started with
the heart
it still beats, and beats, and
beats.

MONOVACIA

I was cast in steel and darkness
and you undid me
and made me over
in blue light

my resurrected hands
undid your belt
and the buttons made of sea-shell
and your flesh reached out to me
like a bridge

and I walked over it
and out of my place of ice
away from the wasteful fire
into your bower

and you were in my body
brother of my heart
and you knew my hunger and my hurt
and you spread under and round me
your swan's wings
your dolphin's love